Parents Ask...

20 Questions
About
Kindergarten

Table of Contents

13. What else do children learn in kindergarten?

14. What role do special support staff and specialists play in the kindergarten classroom?

15. When should I talk to my child's teacher? When should I talk to the principal?

16. What can I do at home to support what my child is doing in school?

17. Why should I get involved with a parent group like the PTA?

18. How do I know if my child is getting a good education and how do I evaluate that?

19. What kinds of special training do kindergarten teachers have?

20. Are all kids ready for first grade after a year of kindergarten? How can I tell if my child is ready?

A (baker's) dozen things to ask your child's kindergarten teacher

5 things to look for in the kindergarten classroom

What is the real purpose of kindergarten?

Just about every American child goes to kindergarten, but the kindergarten experience varies from school to school. There are differences in the approach to teaching and learning; but there are some common themes among kindergarten programs:

- Perhaps most important is the development of self-esteem. This means helping children feel good about who they are; and feeling confident and competent about themselves as they continue in their schooling.
- Also important is the emphasis on cooperation: helping kids learn to work – and get along with others.

- A third common theme is fostering children's natural love of learning — by building on children's curiosity — and helping them learn to express themselves, and communicate and represent their ideas, feelings, and knowledge about the world. Kindergarten helps children discover that learning is fun and meaningful.

How is kindergarten different from preschool? From first grade?

Preschool and child care help children:

- Learn to get along without their parents — sometimes for long periods of the day.
- To relate to other caring adults.
- To socialize with their peers.
- And to learn about themselves and their world through play with different materials.

While play and socialization are still key elements of a kindergarten program, kindergartners are also introduced to more "formal learning" and work in a more organized, independent manner.

In many schools, first grade means an even more structured approach to learning, with less emphasis on play and more on "academic" tasks. Some educators believe, however, that first grade should look and feel more like kindergarten, responding to individual developmental levels of young children.

3 What makes a good kindergarten program?

A good program expands a child's ability to learn about the world, organize information and problem-solve; in turn, this increases feelings of self-worth, confidence, the ability to work with others, and an interest in challenging tasks. Children should feel free to express themselves through talk and through use of blocks, paint, clay, and other creative materials.

A balanced program should also include a combination of formal and informal activities and projects — storytelling, music, dramatic play — which allow children to work in groups and on their own.

Children should be exposed to the written word through meaningful print around the room, books, recipe charts, and seeing their own words recorded.

What to look for:

- Active, hands-on learning.
- A wide variety of materials accessible to children, including: Art; Dramatic Play; Blocks; Science; Writing and drawing materials; Library books; An environment set up for independence; Room for small and large group activity.

Are all five-year-olds "ready" for kindergarten, and what do I do if my child is not quite ready?

No two children develop in precisely the same way or at the same rate. In fact, many educators describe the child's development as having four different dimensions: intellectual, social, emotional, and physical. And they stress that all four of a child's dimensions do not progress or develop at the same rate.

This means that some children may develop more quickly intellectually, while others progress more quickly socially, or physically, or emotionally. All children are individuals who are growing, changing, and learning all the time.

Because different children develop at different rates, they are not all ready for all aspects of kindergarten at the same time. The best schools

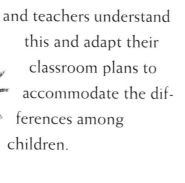

and teachers understand this and adapt their classroom plans to accommodate the differences among children.

If your child's fifth birthday falls near the cutoff date for school admission — and he or she seems unusually immature compared with others her age, or doesn't seem quite ready to learn in a classroom setting — you might consider postponing kindergarten. Most experts recommend waiting a year if you have serious doubts — older children generally do better in school than younger ones.

Do what is best for your child! Make sure your child doesn't feel "stigmatized" or "left back." Talk with the educators in your community, and then make a decision about the best course for your child.

5 What kinds of challenges might come up as my child adjusts to kindergarten, and what's the best way to handle these?

Dealing with separation from parents, adjusting to a new environment, feeling at home, trusting the teacher, making new friends— these are all issues that kindergartners face. The child who has been in day care or preschool — and had positive experiences there — may have an easier time adjusting to kindergarten than a child who has never been away from home before.

But all kindergartners (and their parents!) are encountering a new situation which can cause some anxiety. Don't be surprised if your child — who was well-adjusted at pre-school — suddenly seems less comfortable surrounded by a big

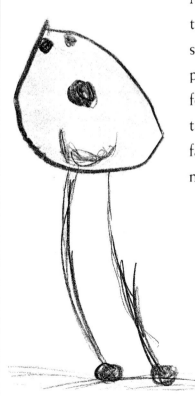

school, big school buses, hallways, a cafeteria, and older kids. Even the fact that your child may have to spend more of the day sitting down may cause anxiety. Indeed, your child may have a hard time separating from you.

Many parents often tend to talk up kindergarten as "real school," and emphasize discipline issues. This can add fear for a child. It is important to talk about what might be familiar and safe, and not just new, big, and important.

To ease the transition, talk to your child in advance about what school will be like. Before school starts, try to make sure that your child gets to play with another child from the same class — both kids will benefit from seeing a familiar face the first day of school.

And if you and the teacher agree that it will be helpful, you may want to stay in the classroom for a while during the first few days of school.

6   What does "developmentally appropriate" mean, anyway—and how does it apply to my school?

Anyone dealing with children should be aware of the various abilities (cognitive, motor, social, intellectual, emotional, etc.) that children develop at each stage of their life. Although every child develops at different rates in different abilities, there are some common patterns that teachers and parents can expect to see at each age.

Educators must make sure that the tasks they ask kids to do — and the materials they provide for children to work with — are in keeping with what can realistically be expected at that age and stage of development. "Developmentally appropriate" activities need to be appropriate for the age group and for the individual. In short, activities should be neither too simple nor too advanced, or children won't benefit from them as fully as they might otherwise.

7 What is the role of play in kindergarten?

When you are five, play is your most important life's work. Children grow and learn through play — especially rich and complex play activities that allow them to solve problems and engage in fantasy.

In kindergarten there should be plenty of time every day for developmentally appropriate group and individual play. Plus it should be play that kids choose and direct themselves.

The classroom should include equipment such as a sandbox and blocks, and special areas such as a "make-believe corner" and "play house" to encourage youngsters to use their imaginations in positive, thought-provoking ways.

8 What will my child learn about reading and writing in kindergarten?

Literacy — the ability to read and write — begins developing at home long before children enter school. Reading and writing develop together, as children gain experience with language and literature. The kindergarten reading and writing program should be an extension of reading and writing that begin at home. (See Question 16 for ways you can help support your child's growing literacy.)

While most kindergarten teachers don't necessarily "teach" reading, in a good program children are immersed in a language-rich environment which helps them to identify words that have meaning to them. Many schools are now taking a "whole language" approach, in which children experience real literature — stories and poems and magazines — rather than reading textbooks or worksheets.

There is naturally a wide range of reading abilities in any one kindergarten class — some children may be fluent readers while others cannot read at all. Parents of non-readers need not worry, as research clearly indicates that children who are formally taught to read in kindergarten have no significant advantage over their peers by the end of second grade.

Writing

In terms of writing, the school program should help children explore ways in which writing is useful and meaningful. Writing may take the form of random or controlled <u>scrib</u>bling, invented spelling (using letters and symbols to represent a word

in their own way), or even a drawing accompanied by words.

Children experiment with different forms of writing to meet their needs and interests. To aid children's explorations, the classroom should provide a variety of writing tools — markers, pens, pencils, crayons, and so on. Children should also have the opportunity to explore different forms of writing such as notes, poems, and journals.

What will my child learn about math?

9

Children begin to understand numbers through measuring, comparing counting and matching quantities. These concepts are reinforced through motor – skills activities such as coloring, pasting, drawing, and the use of special hands-on math materials known as "manipula-tives." These include "table" blocks in a variety of shapes and colors, puzzles, and small objects for sorting, counting, and classifying. Regular building blocks also are a great early-math material for exploring geometry, parts-and-wholes, patterns, and measurement.

10 How will science and social studies be introduced?

While there is often no strict science or social – studies curriculum, in a good kindergarten program, children learn about these subjects through their daily experiences. A good teacher is receptive and sensitive to the children and the science around them.

Young children are naturally curious, and the "study" of science takes place as children investigate and ask questions about the world around them: about the changing seasons; as they examine how things work; when they wonder how animals live; as they ask questions about health.

As children explore, they experiment, they invent, they think about cause and effect, and they predict results.

Children explore properties of materials they are familiar with: sand, water, clay, and paint, among others. For example, as they use blocks, they discover the properties of balance; as they use art materials, they are inventing.

Children explore social studies in much the same way. A good program starts by looking at the lives and cultures of the children and their community. This helps them understand and appreciate who they are, and provides a base from which to look at "larger" communities.

Good programs often help children explore other cultures and places in and thus gain an understanding and appreciation for those who live different lives.

Children learn by looking at pictures, hearing stories, watching videos, and going on field trips. A kindergarten teacher does not dump information on children, but rather teaches through a process of self-discovery.

11 What about art, music, and physical education?

Art and music both play a big role in most kindergarten programs. In addition to giving kids ways to express themselves and exercise their creativity, the arts help build coordination (fine motor skills) and develop literacy, and math and science skills.

Sometimes teacher "specialists" visit the classroom. At other times children visit and work in specialized art or music rooms. In many schools, classroom teachers integrate art and music into their regular kindergarten program.

The kindergarten classroom should have plenty of art supplies, including markers, crayons, finger paints, nontoxic clay, and collage materials for gluing. These should all be accessible for children's daily use. Often, the room will also have a piano or tape recorder, and children will sing songs and play simple instruments.

In terms of physical education, active play helps children learn about the value of exercise as they build their physical strength and muscular coordination. Ideally, the school has an outdoor playground with equipment geared to small children. But some physical – education activities — such as fun dance and creative movement games — work equally well indoors.

12 What will my child learn about getting along with others?

A good early childhood education teacher helps children to work in groups, to play together, to listen to each other, and to become sensitive to one another's feelings.

Kindergartners are very social, and their relationships with peers is very important to them. These relationships can, at times, be very volatile. Consequently, the teacher is also instrumental in showing kids how to resolve their disagreements in a peaceful and positive way. Providing children with the ability to problem-solve — together, in group-time, and independently — is a key piece of kindergarten.

Children learn important social skills and behaviors by interacting with one another in formal and informal activities. Developing these social skills is one of the most important missions of any kindergarten program.

13 What else do children learn in kindergarten?

Once again, it is important to keep in mind that kindergartens vary. But in almost all of them, children learn to express themselves; to listen during discussion time; and to share ideas, items from home, and things they have made. They learn to work together and take responsibility through classroom jobs such as watering plants or helping to pass out snacks.

Children learn to make choices and decisions. They learn the value of quiet time versus active time.

And they develop a sense of themselves and their ability to learn new things all the time.

Children learn about their relationship to the bigger world around them. They are eager to find out how the world works, what the rules are, and how things are made.

What role do special support staff and specialists play in the kindergarten classroom?

Depending on the school, specialists and support staff typically provide a wide range of teaching services. In some schools, subjects such as art, music, and physical education are taught by "specialists." In other schools, these support people refer to psychologists or reading specialists. It is important to ask your child's teacher about the presence and role of these resource professionals.

Specialists typically conduct a wide range of testing with the children — such as evaluating their individual needs or seeking additional information about how a child may best learn.

As a parent, you should be consulted and give your consent before your child is tested. School psychologists often visit the classroom — as a matter of course or at the teacher's request — to observe what's going on and how the children are interacting.

15

When should I talk to my child's teacher? When should I talk to the principal?

When parents and teachers work together as partners, everyone benefits — especially the children. To provide a complete program for children, teachers need to understand how the child interacts at home — and vice versa. Parents need to know what and how their child is doing at school.

To establish an early, positive link with your child's teacher, have a telephone conference or in-person meeting before the school year begins to introduce yourself and set up a partnership. Then keep communication going all year through regular conferences and school visits.

The principal will be most helpful on matters that go beyond the day-to-day activities of the classroom. For example, if there are issues to clear up about school policy, if you are seeking ways to get involved on a schoolwide basis, or if your communications with the teacher have become difficult for some reason, then you should not hesitate to see the principal.

Hopefully, he or she will help you re-establish positive communications with your child's teacher.

16 What can I do at home to support what my child is doing in school?

The three most important things you can do for your kindergartner are:

• First, incorporate reading into your daily routine. Surround your child with age-appropriate books and read to your child each and every day. (See the enclosed poster for a recommended list of books for you and your child to share.) You should also make sure that your child sees you reading.

There are many other things that you can "read" together: cereal boxes, road and store signs, recipes, the everyday print in your surroundings that has meaning to your child.

• Second, show interest in and support of your child's school activities. Encourage your child to talk about school — without "quizzing" — and show that you are listening.

• Third, get involved in your child's play. Invite your child to "write" words or letters or stories to accompany his or her drawings.

Make use of a variety of language experiences through everyday family life: together with your child, make a shopping list, write a telephone message, read names on cereal boxes. Allow your child to express himself or herself with paint, clay, blocks, and other materials, and encourage lots of questions.

Mostly, just take time to talk with your children, and get engaged in their play.

Why should I get involved with a parent group like the PTA?

Parents get involved with the PTA so they can have an active role in their children's education. Some participate when they realize that their children's education is too important to leave in the hands of professionals and politicians alone.

Parents want the best for their children, and theyquickly learn that if they are to have an impact on their children's education, they must work with teachers and administrators to improve their local schools; they can not leave the whole job to them.

School boards and administrators are becoming more aware of "parent power," and are recognizing that the parent really is the child's most important teacher. As a result, schools are increasingly seeking parents' active involvement and partnership.

How do I know if my child is getting a good education and how do I evaluate that?

Listening to your child, asking questions, and observing behavior is the best way to assess the quality of education. Does your child find school fun and satisfying — or is it boring and stressful? Is your child feeling confident and competent?

What kinds of things does your  child talk about doing in school? How are the relationships she or he is forming? Are their strengths as an individual learner being recognized? Is he or she being supported with patience and compassion in areas that need to develop?

These will be good indicators of the kind of education your child is receiving. Do NOT rely on test scores or worksheets coming home as a tool for evaluating your kindergarten program. At the kindergarten level, test scores are neither valid nor reliable, and may give you a misleading picture of how your child is learning and how well the school stacks up against others.

19 What kinds of special training do kindergarten teachers have?

Kindergarten teachers are trained for their work through early childhood education courses at either the undergraduate college or graduate school level. Many are trained to teach other grades as well. Depending on the state, a certificate may be issued specifically for kindergarten teaching, nursery-kindergarten teaching, or a combination of nursery-kindergarten-primary teaching.

In most cases, a kindergarten teacher will have had at least one semester of student teaching — working full-time in a classroom with a licensed teacher — before she or he can be certified.

There is another characteristic that most kindergarten teachers share: a real love of children. As you will quickly see when you visit your child's class, a room full of energetic, curious five-year-olds can challenge even the most dedicated, skilled teacher. But it is the combination of professional skills, experience, and real love that typically turns the kindergarten experience into a joyous one for children.

Are all kids ready for first grade after a year of kindergarten? How can I tell if my child is ready?

It is important to emphasize once more that there is a very wide range of abilities and normal developmental differences among children ages five and six. As a result, not all kids will be equally ready for first grade after one year of kindergarten. Do not assume that your child is not ready just because he or she seems to be less mature in some areas than other kids. It is important to remember that there is a great variability in children's speech development, physical coordination, readiness to sit still, and ability to relate to other children.

If, for example, your child is socially mature but lags in some or all classroom skills, the solution will probably be to advance him or her to first grade — but work with the first – grade teacher to help your child. You and the teacher may decide to provide tutorial or remedial assistance.

If, however, your child seems to be having real difficulty in kindergarten — or if the school has suggested that she or he isn't ready for first grade — you might consider repeating kindergarten or placing your child in a transitional class instead of the regular first grade.

Not surprisingly, there are ramifications for the child, who may believe that he or she has failed and is being punished. It is essential not to damage a child's self – esteem. In short, repeating any grade is a step to be taken only after serious deliberation by both parents and educators. And, not surprisingly, whether or not to repeat a grade is one of the most hotly debated topics among educators.

Whatever your decision, it is crucial that you prepare your child emotionally for what happens next, and lend your full reassurance and support. Repeating kindergarten can be extremely beneficial when a child is truly immature in comparison to classmates. But it should only be done after a full examination of the alternatives with your child's teacher and principal.

A (Baker's) Dozen Things to Ask Your Child's Kindergarten Teacher

1. How many children are in the class? With how many adults? Can I get a list of everyone's names?

2. What are the class rules, school rules, bus rules, playground rules? Is there an established school policy — or booklet — concerning such things as vacations, emergency closing procedures, medical emergencies, and transportation policy?

3. How will the children be welcomed to kindergarten during the first few weeks? Am I expected — or encouraged — to stay, or should I drop my child off?

4. If my child has some problems adjusting or needs some extra help, how will you let me know so I can be part of the solution?

5. How will you handle conflicts between children?

6. How will you handle discipline in the classroom?

7. What's the usual daily routine (nap and snack times, storytelling, etc.)? And how does that routine form the basis — or support — of the curriculum?

8. How much time will children spend learning in groups, and how much time working independently?

9. Will my child be given things to do at home? If so, how can I help my child?

10. What special events and field trips do you have planned? How can I participate?

11. If my child is not feeling well in the morning — or was sick the night before — when should I keep my child home? What happens if my child gets sick at school?

12. What's the best way for you and me to keep in touch? When can I reach you by phone?

13. When can I visit the classroom? How can I help — in the classroom and outside?